FINDING THE
GOODNESS OF
God

SABRINA WAGES

Trilogy Christian Publishers
A Wholly Owned Subsidiary of Trinity Broadcasting Network
2442 Michelle Drive
Tustin, CA 92780

For information, address Trilogy Christian Publishing
Rights Department, 2442 Michelle Drive, Tustin, Ca 92780.
Trilogy Christian Publishing/ TBN and colophon are trademarks
of Trinity Broadcasting Network.
For information about special discounts for bulk purchases,
please contact Trilogy Christian Publishing.
Manufactured in the United States of America

10 9 8 7 6 5 4 3 2 1
Library of Congress Cataloging-in-Publication Data is available.
ISBN 978-1-63769-428-2
ISBN 978-1-63769-429-9 (ebook)

Dedication

This book is dedicated to my Lord and Savior, Jesus Christ. You are my one true love, my hope, and my future—my everything.

Acknowledgements

First and above all, I would like to thank my Lord and Savior Jesus Christ for the inspiration and words that you will find in this book. While the adventure itself isn't one that I would've chosen, it is what I will always remember as a true journey of hope, peace, joy, and finding my true identity in Him.

While I know that God did not give me cancer, I do believe I was allowed to walk this journey because He knew I had faith to overcome. Through this journey I found my true identity in Him, and discovered just how amazing my faith truly is!

I want to thank the Lord for each and every word written in this book. I prayed so much during it and believed that I would write what He spoke to me, to impact others in a way that my natural self can't. I don't wish for others to hear me, but to hear Him.

So Lord, I come before you today and thank you for all that you've done and are going to do. I thank you for the words here and ask that they impact the reader in a way they've never been impacted before. Lead them closer to you and wrap your arms of love around them all day and everyday of the rest of their lives. Amen.

To my amazing mom, without you I don't know where I'd be. You are a true inspiration and have already changed more lives than my own. You are who I aspire to be and your faith shines brighter than I think you'll ever know or understand. You are beautiful, inside and out. You are an anointed world changer, so go change the world!

To Brother Moore and Mrs. Moore, thank you for all the faith-filled teachings over the years. Without those I would've been so lost in this season where my faith was tested in ways I never knew it could be. Thank you for following the Word of the Lord all those years ago and for truly fulfilling your calling.

To Mrs. Kim, you are a strong woman of faith who already fought and won a battle similar to mine. Thank you for being there for me and saying just what I needed to hear when I needed to hear it. You are a true inspiration to me and words will never express my thanks to you. To me, you are another mama in my life and I'm not sure you truly understand the impact you had on me during this season and before. You will always hold a special place in my heart and our bond is one that can never be broken. Love you, Mrs. Kim.

Brother Dave, you always say the right words at the right time and have become such a father figure in my life. Thank you for your love and kindness that you've shown me all my days.

To my amazing sisters and brothers, I don't know where I'd be without your love and support. Thank you for the constant giggles and for sharing your hearts with me.

To Mike and Shara, I don't know what I'd do without you. You both have become such an intricate part of my life and for that I am so thankful. Words will never be able to express my gratitude for you.

To Mrs. Susan, you always make me smile with your smile. You can brighten anyone's day with a quick glance, I am so thankful for you. Thank you for always being there for me and for standing by me throughout a tough season. Your kindness did not go unseen, and I will be thankful for you all of my days.

To my grandparents, Mel and Kathy, thank you for your strength, love, and support during this challenging season. I love you beyond words.

To Karissa, thank you for making me laugh and keeping me company on our girls days. You always know just what to say and when to keep quiet and let me vent. You mean the world to me!

Crystal, thank you for being so open and honest with me about all that you've been through. I couldn't have gone through this season without you.

Jessica C., thank you for your love and support through all

of this. Your smile always lights up the room. Your love is always felt when I'm around you, texting you, talking with you, or simply thinking about you. Keep being your strong, sweet self and shining brightly for Him.

Table of Contents

Preface

My hope for you is that throughout this book you find encouragement, regardless of where you are in life right now. Whether you've had a cancer diagnosis, you're believing for something big, you don't know how you'll continue, or you're in the best spot you've ever been in—I hope you find encouragement in the words of the Lord.

I've wanted to write a book for a while on the goodness of God, but it wasn't until I was diagnosed with cancer in 2020 and truly saw the goodness of God in more ways than I ever had before that I got very inspired to write this book.

I knew God was good, but there comes a time in everyone's life where they are faced with a decision to follow God or be mad at Him. This was one of those choices I had to make.

I knew I had to follow Him with every part of my being. I knew I had to embrace Him and let Him embrace me. I knew that I had no choice but to follow God through whatever this journey brought because He is good. He's nothing but good. He can only do good. So why would I choose any other path than the one He lays before me?

Truth be told, I'm in tears as I write this because God has been so faithful to me. He has shown me that I can trust in Him all the days of my life and all He will continue to do is good. My heart aches at the thought of thinking anything else.

Follow me on this journey as I tell the story of God's goodness to me. I encourage you to read every word, even if you've never had cancer. We all have choices to make in this life and I hope that you always choose to follow the goodness of God.

If you had asked me two years ago if I would be fighting cancer in 2020, I would've laughed. I'm a healthy twenty-four year old girl, who would even think that would happen to someone like me?

Well, come to 2020 and you'll see that it did. I was diagnosed September fourth with Hodgkins Lymphoma. This was after having a splenectomy (spleen removal surgery) on September 1st. Even the surgeon was almost positive that it wasn't cancer, he was sure it would be sarcoidosis and easily treatable with a round of steroids.

When I first got the diagnosis, I wasn't scared. There were just so many unknowns when it came to treatments and the path to take. What wasn't unknown was God and the faith I have in Him.

He is my mighty Savior and no one is greater than Him. He is my constant, my ever help in trouble. I can't even begin to express the gratitude and thanks I have for Him throughout this season and the ones to come.

This is my story, my story of overcoming. My story of finding peace through a time of tribulation. My story of finding strength during this season of conquering. My story of the God who loves me and how He won this battle for me. This, is my story.

Finding Hope in the Darkness

Through this journey I had times of doubt. Not in God, but in the situations and circumstances that surrounded me. In a world that is fallen and for the most part brings heartache to those around it and in it.

No one wants to hear the words "You have cancer." No one. I have yet to meet someone who wanted to hear those words.

When I was initially told, I was in a hospital all by myself. It was in April of 2020, so COVID-19 was a thing and so were lockdowns. Therefore no one could be with me. Here I am, twenty-three years old in an ER and after only two hours of testing the doctor says, "Call your mom." So, with my mom on speaker phone, he proceeds to tell me that what they found can only be cancer. He wants to do more testing of course, but it can only be that.

I spent three and a half days in the hospital waiting for the biopsy that no one ordered until the third day. I had the biopsy along with a bone marrow biopsy and neither could confirm their diagnosis.

So we waited. We waited three months and proceeded to do another PET scan that showed them something they didn't like. So we met with a surgeon to do a more invasive, surgical biopsy. He didn't like the idea of doing a surgery just to rule something out, so instead he wanted to biopsy my enlarged spleen that had been an area of concern. In order to biopsy a spleen, it must be removed. So after a bit of prayer and time spent with God, we agreed and scheduled the surgery.

After four days in the hospital, there I laid, without a spleen. I was fine, you can live without it. It's only about twenty percent of your immune system and is a common organ to have removed throughout one's life. However, there I laid, and the surgeon comes in and asks me to call my mom (who again is not with me due to covid). He then tells me that they found Hodgkins Lymphoma and would recommend treatment as soon as they could start.

Hearing all of this wasn't what I wanted to hear. It's not what anyone wants to hear. However, in both of those moments as those doctors told me what they found, I had a choice. Give in to fear or give in to God.

In that moment, the feeling of fear smacks you like a ton of bricks. It can overwhelm you to a point of breaking that only a few have known or experienced. That's all it is though, a feeling. It's not a deciding factor, it's not what chooses for you. It's a feeling. We don't have to live by feelings. We, as Christians, can choose to live by faith.

As the first doctor left my hospital room, I spoke out plain as day to my mom and told her, "I will not fear." In that moment, those are the words that came up so strong in my heart. From all I'd heard growing up in a faith church, I knew what I spoke first mattered. I knew that the initial words that came out of my mouth would make a world of difference.

I chose in that moment to overcome my fear with faith. I knew that somehow, someway, God was making this right. Let me make one thing super clear here, God did not give me this disease. In no way, shape, or form did it come from Him. God is good and can only do good. This was straight-up from the devil. We live in a fallen world where Satan is the god, and he sucks. Just saying.

Anyway, faith was my only true and honest choice in that moment. I knew that if I chose to give this over to God that He would take care of me.

As I laid in that hospital bed both times, my faith grew. It does that when you lay there with no other choice in the world but to truly toss all of your cares upon the Lord and let Him handle what you are going through.

Things play over in your head and you have to put an end to them. The devil is a clever guy and knows just how to penetrate you to make you cave, but you don't have to. The grace and peace of God is so much stronger in you than anything the puny devil could throw.

God is strength, and when He lives inside of you, that strength does too. So, when the devil throws thoughts of doubt and confusion your way, remember that the God who made the planets lives inside of you. You have the almighty not only fighting your battles, but giving you the strength to fight too.

I chose that day not to fear but to have faith in the God of heaven. The God of love. The God of abundance. The God of healing. The God of strength. I chose to hand over what the world would say is a "big problem" to a God who is bigger— to a God who adores me and wants only the best for me.

I'll be honest, laying in the hospital bed after the first "diagnosis," I had a rough go. I got frustrated more than once because no one had put in the order to do the biopsy. I couldn't have any visitors due to covid. My sweet mama was just sitting outside in her car all day every day just so I knew she was there. There were moments I wasn't in true faith and I'll be the first one to truly admit that.

I never doubted my healing or God, but I got frustrated with the way the world around me was operating and at the fact that I couldn't control any of it.

I had a sweet faith buddy, friend, and mentor from church call me while I laid there and remind me kindly that frustration isn't faith. Let's just say that snapped me out of my funk pretty quick. I regained my composure and began to see things in a new light. I began to see things as God sees them and started to stand strong instead of like a little wilted flower that kept getting stepped on.

I chose to gather any and all the strength I had in me to fight this battle that I personally couldn't win. My God could and was going too though. I knew it deep down that no matter what, I was going to win. Not by my own strength, but His. Not by anything I could do, but by everything that He could.

Truly Seeing God's Goodness

Finding God's goodness in the midst of a battle is easier than it seems. When we live in this world that is so full of hatred and evil, we sometimes tend to see only the negative in our lives, not the positive. To us, it's easier to let our thoughts wander to the people who hurt us, the things that aren't going right, or the circumstances that seem to have devastated our lives.

Finding God's goodness through all of it is a choice. It's a daily decision to open our eyes to the truth and see all the glorious things that our God has done for us despite what is happening around us.

Throughout my journey I have been faced many times with this choice. Through tests (and more tests), through treatments of chemo, and especially through the financial needs that arise during it all.

I wasn't given a choice in walking this path. Once I found out I was diagnosed with this (I will always refer to it as being diagnosed with because I never "had" it and *by golly* it never had me), the only choice I had was chemo or no chemo. Before I was diagnosed, I had a choice of whether to do the dozen or so tests or not. Ultimately though, it wasn't really a choice. These tests needed to be done and the chemo did too.

I'm not saying there aren't times the Lord says not to do some of these things. There was one test (a surgical lymph node biopsy) that the oncologist wanted me to have done back in May, shortly after all of this began, that we didn't feel led to do. Now, we spent a lot of time in prayer regarding that choice and had others believe with us that we would have the wisdom we needed. When we approached the oncologist he was at peace with that choice and asked me to do another PET scan in three months, which I did.

All of that to say, be led. Everyone is different and you must ultimately make the decision the Lord has for you. Medicine is not bad though, and sometimes the route of doctors is the route you should take. It doesn't mean you're not in faith and it doesn't mean you aren't trusting God. Ultimately, the doctors have the same goal as God, to get you well.

What we must choose to see first off is that God did not do the bad things to us. This is a fallen world and bad is all around. In 2 Corinthians 4:4 (NLT) we read,

Satan, who is the god of this world, has blinded the minds of those who don't believe. They are unable to see the glorious light of the Good News. They don't understand this message about the glory of Christ, who is the exact likeness of God.

This shows us clearly that Satan is the god of this world. If you read back in Genesis, once Adam and Eve ate from the fruit of the tree of the knowledge of good and evil, the tree that God distinctly said not to eat from, the world fell. It became a fallen world and God's hand was taken off of it.

Don't go getting mad at Adam and Eve. I've found myself tempted to be like, "Hey, why'd you go messing things up for us?" However, if we're being completely honest, some-one would've messed it up at some point. It could've as easily been you and me. That's a side effect of God's graciousness to give us free will. We can choose right all the days of our life, but we also have the option to choose wrong.

Now we must choose each day to ask God to put His hand back on it. Ask Him to put His hand of protection, love, peace, joy, and so much more back on our lives and the lives of those around us.

The Lord so graciously wants that. He wants to protect us from everything that could possibly harm us and to wrap His arms around us tight and never let us go. He's our Father. The best one out there. We have to ask Him though. We have to invite Him into our lives and open the door for him. He's a gentleman, He won't just barge right in.

This is why we must make a conscious effort everyday to

find the goodness in the world around us. There are so many things we have to be thankful for, despite what is going on. When we choose to focus on the good things, we open up our minds and lives to a whole new world. We've swung that door wide open in an endeavor to invite the truly amazing creator of the universe to do even more good in our lives.

He amazes me daily at how much good He has already done in my life, and then as I open my eyes to that, He does even more. This world we live in may be fallen, but it's a beautiful, beautiful place when we realize how much good is in it because God is in it.

Satan may be the god of this world, but God still has His hand in it showing off to those that will follow Him. It really all comes down to a choice.

With what I walked through last year and into this one, I could've chosen to see only the negative. I could've chosen to say that my life sucks, complain, and wonder why this is happening to me. I made a choice though too view only the goodness of God in each and every circumstance that arose. I chose to see His goodness in it all despite how I "felt." It's a conscious effort on any of our parts to open up our hearts to Him and open up our eyes to the amazing things going on around us.

Think about today, what good things did He do for you just today? Did He give you a front parking spot at the grocery store? That's the goodness of God. Did He give you fifty percent off that blouse you've been wanting? This is the goodness of God. Did He provide a way for something where no other way was possible? Goodness of God. Did He give you peace of mind when all you wanted to do was explode? That's all the goodness of God.

Just remember that it's always a choice. It's your choice on whether you see the goodness of God or not. It's there, you just need to open your heart, mind, and eyes and see it.

Living in the Overflow of Blessings

Through a season of medical fun, one can lose sight of the blessings around them. It's too easy to get caught up in what you can't do or have, that it's very easy to focus solely on that instead of what you do have. What you can do.

Throughout this journey, I have had to be more cautious than most. I wear my mask everywhere (but who doesn't right now haha). I sanitize my hands often and wipe down things I will touch. I stay home a little more than I used to and nap more right now.

Back when I had my first informational meeting on chemo, I cried. Just being one hundred percent honest and real, I cried. Honestly, most of the crying had to do with the fact that they said I would lose my hair (which I didn't) than what I couldn't do. However, they had also told me that I couldn't hug people through it because of the germs. They also said that when I went to church I should be late coming and leave early. This almost broke me, for real. I don't live in fear of germs, never have and never will, but hearing all these things I couldn't do made my heart ache.

We already lived in a time where hugging was limited and they wanted to take it away completely. That's how I took it at least. It took me a bit of time to overcome this obstacle and find the balance of listening to the doctors and not living in fear but in faith. It actually took the words of our co-pastor to snap me out of it. His wife had gone through chemo a few years back so he knew all about it. I asked him where the line was between walking in faith and obeying the doctors.

He then told me that he kept his wife home after treatments too and if I didn't feel well that I can always stay home and watch online. He explained that since chemo's goal is to go in and wipe out all the cells and then rebuild, one does have to be more careful during this time.

It's not lack of faith, it's respect to your own body and taking care of you. Throughout the months that followed I was extra cautious but didn't stop living my life. I took it day by day and knew when I needed to stay home or nap a little extra.

During this time though I was able to find so many blessings when I looked for them. Some I didn't even have to look that hard for. I had friends show up with special treats just for me. People texted me all the time just to check on me or encourage me. On treatment days I had so many people to text back and forth while I sat there.

I got hugs all the time (I did break this rule that the doctors asked of me because there was no way I was going six months with no hugs - I did typically have my mask on though just to be safe). People blessed me with goodie baskets full of comfort items. I got to go out and have girls days and coffee with friends I hadn't gotten to just sit and talk with in a while.

Financial blessings began to flow into my life and money just gets handed to me all the time. I did add that to my daily confessions! It works guys! Our words work.

As I really looked and thought about everything that happened during this time, I truly saw the overflow of blessings in my life. I had a choice to make though in cultivating a heart of thankfulness so that I was more aware of these blessings.

Our words have such a big part to play in being blessed. Living in the overflow of blessings requires us to maintain a positive lifestyle and keep speaking only words of life, not death, out of our mouth.

Proverbs 18:21 (KJV) says that "life and death are in the power of the tongue." This verse speaks volumes into how much we can and should use our words to be a world changer for us. In Deuteronomy 30:19 (NIV), it says that "God laid before us life and death, choose life." He told us what to choose! He made it that easy by simply telling us what to choose, we just have to actually do it.

When we use our words negatively, we are only hurting ourselves. If you read James 3, it talks about how a small rudder steers a whole ship and that a small bit controls a giant horse. It compares our tongue to that rudder and bit, explaining that what we say can control and change our whole lives.

When we speak positively, we give God something to work with. We open the door to Him and invite Him in to do miraculous wonders in our lives.

During my medical journey, I chose each day to use my words to bring life into my body. I had so much to stand against. The disease in my body for one. The cancer had to go in the name of Jesus!

Then, there was the weight loss I had experienced. I started 2020 at one hundred fourteen pounds, and by April 1st was ninety-seven pounds. That was one thing they truly wanted me to watch during my treatments, eating. They wanted to make sure I didn't lose anymore. Throughout the journey of beginning treatment, I began to gain that weight back. It took a bit, but I did it! On my last chemo treatment, March 5, 2021, I am pleased to say that I hit one hundred fourteen pounds once again! Praise the Lord! That is a testimony in itself that I gained weight during chemo. It was truly a blessing of the Lord!

I also had the possibility of the chemo drug side affects. I knew all about them, we sat through a hour and half meeting of all the possible side effects that the drugs could do. Those meetings you must go into with solid faith, no fear, or they will determine how you do during your chemo treatments. Personally, I'm so thankful that I went through that meeting with the Lord and my mother right there beside me. I didn't let any of it get in me, and I truly believe that changed the course of my chemo. I didn't experience any negative side effects. I never threw up, my taste changed slightly for a day or two after treatments maybe five or six, then they went back to normal. I was a little sleepy but nothing a nap couldn't fix. Within two-three days I was my normal, bubbly self!

On top of all the physical things to overcome, I had the emotional "battle" within. So much to overcome on that front. I can't even begin to express all the emotions that come with this sort of thing, but it's a lot. However, our God is more. God is the only reason I came through this the way I did. He helped me overcome so many thoughts and feelings (so thankful we don't live by those). To God be all the glory, forever and ever.

My faith through this got so much stronger. I don't doubt for a second that my God is good and will do only good for me. The devil messed up big time. I drew so much closer to God during this time and will continue to use this experience as a testimony of how great my God is. I will declare God's goodness for all the days of my life.

At the end of the book is a list of my daily confessions I spoke over myself. These can be repeated just as they are, or modified to cover exactly what you are going through right now. God is good and faithful to fulfill all His promises to us!

So, overflow of blessings? They're there, you just have to look. Open your eyes and see all the incredibly amazing things that God has fulfilled in your life. Only then can He begin to do even more.

♪

Faith for Finances

This is something that I hesitate to share because people stand in different places on finances. However, my God is a God that supplies all my needs according to *His* riches in glory by Christ Jesus, and I want you to know that He will do it for you too (see Philippians 4:19, NIV)!

Anything medical normally brings something financial along with it. Even with insurance, the bills come while insurance figures out what they'll pay. I have grown so much in the area of faith for finances that I almost can't believe it.

When I began getting the bills, I would falter some. Just being completely honest and truthful with you. I would look at those huge numbers and wonder if it was all worth it (just so you know, it's just money and yes your life is more than worth it) and how it would all come to pass as paid for. I knew God could do it, no doubt there, but I would wander into the thought realm of how it would be done.

Let me start by putting Isaiah 55:8-9 (NIV) here for you to read.

"For my thoughts are not your thoughts, neither are your
ways my ways," declares the Lord. "As the heavens are
higher than the earth, so are my ways higher than your ways
and my thoughts than your thoughts."

God does not think or act like we do, praise the Lord. If He did, I'm not sure what I'd do because I'm pretty sure at times I'd be doomed. But, there is that saving grace that God is so much higher and different than all of us. You have no idea how at ease that puts my heart.

For me personally, I did have insurance. However, my insurance deemed my elevated white blood cell count as a pre-existing condition and wanted to deny every claim. I got that news right as I was beginning treatment, as well as the info from them that they don't cover chemo at all. Now I had a choice to make, give up or give it to God. I chose to give it to God.

While I also qualified for Medicaid, that was a four month process and even though it finally kicked in, there were still months of unpaid bills. I went to the financial department at the hospital and they have been unbelievably nice and on my side. It's truly a blessing to have them.

In reference to all that I named above, I want to touch base on one thing. You must do your part of the harvest. In Matthew 9:37 (NIV) we read where God says, "The harvest is plentiful but the workers are few." We have a part to play in our harvest coming in. The amount of phone calls and times I sat on hold to get my medical journey paid for was a lot. I mean a lot. However, it was necessary. There were times I would get frustrated (which isn't faith, I know) and times I would even cry. God took care of it though. He provided all along the way and continues to this day.

He opened so many doors of opportunity for me. One of the big ones is that I was granted a wish from the Nikolas Ritschel Foundation. Through them, I was able to arrange for my family to meet Michael Tait (the lead singer for Newsboys) and attend his concert this fall, as well as have an all expense paid trip to Maine. This blessing is one that I will never forget and God made it all possible through this amazing organization.

Throughout it all, I had to constantly remind myself that God supplies all my needs according to His riches in glory by Christ Jesus. Not according to my riches or the worlds, but His. How amazing is that?

This is another thing that I added to my daily confessions. I needed to not only keep the reminder right in front of me, but open the door for God to be able to walk through and take care of it.

God took and continues to take care of me, and He'll do the exact same thing for you. I remember Jesse Duplantis talking about when he'd get bills in the mail, he'd hold them up and say, "Jesus, you've got mail!" So hold up whatever is pressing on you today and simply say, "Jesus."

When You Want to Give Up

※

First of all, I want to say that when you want to give up, don't. Simple as that—I know, maybe not so simple. However, it can be!

God is so good and has help me overcome so much. I can honestly say I never wanted to give up per se during this medical journey, but there were times when I really wanted to be done. I knew I'd overcome the treatments with flying colors and I was already cancer free, but I was so ready to not have any more chemicals put into my body.

The first step to overcoming the want to give up is knowing and trusting in God completely. Do not listen to anyone around you that would say otherwise. If that means you need to surround yourself with constant praise music and faith preaching for days on end, do it. You need to have the Word of God so deeply rooted in you that nothing else can creep in and tell you something other than God is good.

If anyone in the Bible had a reason to give up it'd be Noah. It hadn't rained ever where he was from. People ridiculed, laughed, and mocked him. He was building a big boat that took over one hundred years to build, which means he took that ridicule and mockery for that long. By earthly standards, Noah had every reason to give up, but he didn't. He chose to follow the One who had given him the words to begin with and trust that God would bring all that He said to pass.

A wise woman once told me, "During treatments I would sometimes stand at the kitchen sink and cry. Then, I would get myself together and move on. Just because I had a moment doesn't mean I wasn't in faith." This woman is such an inspiration to me and I don't know if she'll ever know how much she's changed my life.

We're human, we have moments where the thoughts come about how we will make it or what we will do next. This, however, is where we have the choice of choosing God over those thoughts. Romans 12:2 (ESV) says to "be transformed by the renewing of your mind." It says to let God transform us into a new being.

In order to do so, we must draw close to Him, allowing Him into our hearts so that the transformation of our minds can begin. When we begin to change the way we think, we begin to see the world as God sees it. It opens up our minds to see the good around us and to focus on that instead of all the negative of the world.

God has such amazing things planned for us, as you can read in Jeremiah 29:11 (NIV). He has plans to prosper us, not to harm us. To give us hope and a future. Being that God can only do good, that means that our future is bright and good.

Giving up should never be an option for those grounded in the faith of our Lord and Savior Jesus Christ. Our view should only be on Him and all that He has for us. When we solely focus on the One above, we can easily cancel out all the negativity going on around us. It helps us to keep our sights on Him.

Second Timothy 4:17 (NIV) says, "But the Lord stood at my side and gave me strength." I almost teared up when I read this. When you feel like you can't go on anymore, picture this. The Lord, the almighty God, the Creator of the universe is standing right beside you. He reaches over to you, lifts you up, and gives you His strength as he whispers, "Go on, I've got you." How incredibly amazing is that?

When we think we can't go on, our greatest cheerleader, God, is telling us otherwise. He has open arms for us to jump into and then uses those same, strong arms, to push us up, and lift us through all of our trials.

A major part of staying on top of keeping our focus on God is our words. Our words are more powerful than I think most realize. Proverbs 21:23 (ESV) says, "Whoever keeps his mouth and his tongue keeps himself out of trouble." Calamity is best described as an event causing great disaster. So, our words have the power to cause great damage. Therefore, our words also have the power to cause great blessings in our lives.

There are two sides to this. The world we live in has good

and evil. The same can be said for the words we speak. If they can cause bad things, they can be used as force for great amounts of good too.

It is so important in our society nowadays to be the ones who speak confidently in the direction of good. There are so many that focus on the negative, we must use our words to influence the world for good.

By doing so, this builds up not only those around us but the spirit within us. It allows God to enter into every area of our lives that we choose to speak life into. As this builds us up, we don't give into the thoughts of giving up so easily.

When we change our focus to God, we see the way that He thinks and responds instead of the way the world thinks and responds. When our perspective changes to God's perspective, we will no longer want to give up because we can then see all the good things He has in store for us.

Look to Him today and focus solely on His will and His way, only then can we live a life of not wanting to give up. We actually turn to a life of wanting to strive and do more for those around us, and continue seeking His plan for us so that we can accomplish all he has for us down here.

Seeing the Love Around You

You are loved. I just wanted to start by making that so abundantly clear. The God of the universe, the one who made the stars and knows how many hairs are on your head, loves you.

John 3:16 (NIV) even says, "For God so loved the world that He gave His only begotten son…" Just the fact that God's heart gave up His only son to be scarified for you and me should be enough to show us His love for all eternity.

However, He didn't stop there. He continues to love our broken selves every day. (In the back of the book I have listed scriptures for each chapter, so you will find lots of them on love back there.)

First Peter 4:8 (NIV) says, "Above all, love each other deeply, because love covers over a multitude of sins." No matter how badly you mess up or what you do, when we repent, we open the door for God to love us so much that His love spills over and covers our sins. How incredible is that?

I want to talk about a key component in seeing the love

in the world around you and truly being able to love like the Lord. My reference is found in Mark 12:31 (NIV), which says,

The second is this: 'Love your neighbor as yourself.' There is no commandment greater than these.

I have heard this scripture for years, but it was only a few years ago that I saw a new, raw perspective of this verse. The Lord showed it to me one day and I've never thought of it the same again.

In this verse we read, "love your neighbor," and I feel like so many people stop there. I know I did. Love those around you, those the Lord puts in your path. This is something you are taught from a young age, especially when you grow up in the church.

It was the second part of the verse that truly caught my eye a few years ago—"As yourself…" As myself? Wait, I'm supposed to love myself too? Isn't that selfish? Conceited maybe?

When you read this verse together though, it says, "love your neighbor as yourself." So, what does that mean? I'm so glad you asked! In order to love our neighbor the way that God intended, we must first be aware of how to love ourselves. Without this knowledge, we can't truly love our neighbor.

Then, we come to the question of how do I love myself? Well, the answer can be found in 1 John 4:7 (NIV), which says,

Dear friends, let us love one another, for love comes from God. Everyone who loves has been born of God and knows God.

Our love comes from God. We find the correct way to love others and ourselves by learning how God loves.

This is how God showed his love among us: He sent his one and only Son into the world that we might live through him. This is love: not that we loved God, but that he loved us and sent his Son as an atoning sacrifice for our sins. Dear friends, since God so loved us, we also ought to love one another.

—1 John 4:9-11 (NIV)

True love is knowing that God loves us. We can love Him through all our human mistakes and errors, but knowing that God loves us through all of that, there is true love. He loves us despite what we may say or do that isn't just right.

We should strive daily to be more like Him though. To be selective with our words and actions, doing only His will and His way. Our words have death or life in them, we can literally change our world with what we say. Which is why we must be so careful with what comes out of our mouths.

God knows we mess up though, and loves us through it. We just have to say a simple "Lord, forgive me," be truly sorry, and ready to change. I don't know about you, but this sounds like true love to me.

So, how does this relate to loving yourself? It's simple... once we find how God loves us, we can love ourselves properly, and only then can we truly love others with the heart of love God has given to us. Let's look at a few attributes of love.

> The Lord appeared to us in the past, saying: "the Lord appeared to him from far away. I have loved you with an everlasting love; therefore I have continued my faithfulness to you."
>
> —Jeremiah 31:3 (ESV)

An attribute of love is faithfulness. We read here that God loves us with an everlasting love, then He says that He continues His faithfulness to us. The two are so linked together. If you love, you're faithful to the end.

Another attribute of love is being slow to anger.

> But you, O Lord, are a God merciful and gracious, slow to anger and abounding in steadfast love and faithfulness. When one is slow to anger, they are walking in true love. God is slow to anger with us, which is why we must extend that to our neighbors and everyone we meet in this life.
>
> —Psalm 86:15 (NIV)

Abounding in love is abounding in patience. When you are

patient with those around you and process before getting mad, you are shining God's light and illuminating a dark world with His glorious light.

> I have been crucified with Christ. It is no longer I who live, but Christ who lives in me. And the life I now live in the flesh I live by faith in the Son of God, who loved me and gave himself for me.

> — Galatians 2:20 (NIV)

Christ gave Himself for us, the ultimate act of love. When we extend the same kindness to our brothers and sisters in Christ or not, we are showing an act of true love just like Jesus did when He died on that cross.

This doesn't just mean giving your life for someone. This includes giving up things, sacrificing for the sake of someone other than yourself. Maybe you wanted the last piece of pie, but so did they and you willingly gave the pie to them. That's sacrifice. I know it sounds silly, saying that giving up a piece of pie is anything like giving your life. However, when one crucifies their flesh in order to give to someone else, that is true sacrifice. Putting someone else's needs above your own is what true love is all about. Living in sacrifice is living in love.

> But because of his great love for us, God, who is rich in mercy, made us alive with Christ even when we were dead in transgressions—it is by grace you have been saved.

> —Ephesians 2:4-5 (NIV)

45

Mercy is another attribute of pure love. When we show others mercy where they don't deserve it, we are showing true love. When they deserve something be done by world standards, but we choose to turn the other cheek and give mercy, we give love.

When we're able to demonstrate the love I've talked about to others, we are able to see more clearly when that love is shown to us. Being able to recognize the attributes of love opens up our eyes to see the truest of loves around us. Only then, can we also see the love that the Father of heaven so lavishly shines down on us.

Being Embraced By the Love of God

Have you ever longed to feel safe? Longed to know how it truly feels to be encompassed with love itself? Have you ever wanted to know a place that nothing else matters and you truly feel the greatest peace ever known?

I'm here to tell you today that that kind of place exists. The kind of place that so many in this world dream about. The kind of place that some believe is only achievable in fairy tales. A love that to the world makes no sense in the way of how someone could love that much.

A scripture that represents this so well is found in Psalm 91:1,4 (NIV),

> Whoever dwells in the shelter of the Most High will rest in the shadow of the Almighty… He will cover you with his feathers, and under his wings you will find refuge; his faithfulness will be your shield and rampart.

This right here. This is that amazing place of love that our hearts have longed for for so long. That place where we can be ourselves and know that all we'll receive in return is love. The place where we aren't judged for being us, but loved for being our one of a kind selves. A place where our hearts long to be.

Now, how do we get to this incredibly amazing place? If you read down in verse nine (NIV), it says "If you say, 'The Lord is my refuge,' and you make the Most High your dwelling." We must invite Him in. Like I said in a previous chapter, God is a gentleman. He isn't going to barge in where He isn't welcome.

The first step to this is being saved and inviting Him into our hearts. In the back of this book you'll find the call to salvation. It doesn't take long, but when said from a place of true intent and pure love for our Lord, it is the most amazing and personal thing you'll ever experience. Not to mention the most vital event of your existence. When we invite God in and He lives in us, only then can we truly know the love that He has for us.

> But may all who seek you rejoice and be glad in you; may those who long for your saving help always say, "The Lord is great!"
>
> —Psalm 70:4 (NIV)

Seeking God opens up the door for so much more than the love of God, which ultimately is enough to make your heart swell with joy for your entire life. Psalm 103:2 (NIV) says, "Praise the Lord, my soul, and forget not all his benefits." So, when we invite Him in, we get more than just an unforgettable love.

> …who forgives all your sins and heals all your diseases, who redeems your life from the pit and crowns you with love and compassion, who satisfies your desires with good things so that your youth is renewed like the eagle's.
>
> —Psalm 103: 3-5 (NIV)

Whoa, we get alot more! He forgives us all our sins, this right here is world changing. Raise your hand if you've never sinned! Okay, no one should have their hand raised unless you're Jesus. So, this definitely benefits us all. Every day before we lay our head on the pillow, we should make sure to repent for every sin that day, to start clean with a new slate the next day. That's why I love Lamentations 3:22-23 (NIV) that say His mercies are new every morning. To know that if I mess up, He forgives and gives me mercy is such an incredible feeling.

He heals all your diseases. This includes everything from a scratch on your hand to a terminal disease, plus everything in between. He doesn't pick and choose, He heals all.

He redeems our life from the pit. What pit is He talking about? Won't we all just go to heaven when this life is over with? The answer to that is no. He redeems us from the fall that occurred when Adam and Eve ate from the tree of the knowledge of good and evil. He opens up a new way for us, to save us from going down into the pit of hell forever. Thank goodness for a truly loving God!

He crowns us with love and compassion… Oh how sweet that is to say! When we give our lives to God, He plants all of the things we need in this life in us. When we need to love someone with the love He gives, it's already there. When someone needs to be shown the compassion that only God can give, it's in our hearts to spread to the world. He instills in us what we need. It's there—we just have to open up our hearts to share it.

That last part of that verse says that He satisfies our desires, which is near and dear to my heart. We can get so consumed in this world with what we need to do that we can sometimes forget that God has every intent to fulfill the desires of our hearts as well.

He wants us to open up to Him and share with Him what we desire to do, to be, and to have. He placed those desires in our hearts for a reason. He wants us to overcome any fear that may be there and have those things that we desire. If He put a desire in your heart, it was for a very good reason. He wants you to utilize that desire and allow Him to fulfill it in your life.

He longs to see His creation happy because we are His children. Parents want their children happy, it's what makes their world go around. So open up your heart and let Him fulfill every desire in it that's just waiting to come out.

One of the truest and strongest desires the Lord has is for

us to know how loved we are. He wants us to understand how wide, how long, how amazing, and how unstoppable His love is for us. His hearts desire is for you to know that love all the days of your life.

Open up your heart today to the love of Jesus Christ. Open it to know the love of a God that so desperately wants to penetrate every heart in the world today. Let love in and you'll never know a time without it again.

You Matter and God Has a Plan for You

L et's start by reading Jeremiah 29:11 (NIV), which says,

"For I know the plans I have for you," declares the Lord,
"plans to prosper you and not to harm you, plans to give you
hope and a future."

This is such a powerful verse to all who are saved, and an amazing hope and encouragement to those who are not. For those of us who are saved, this opens the door to a future of opportunity. Not the opportunities we see in our future, but the ones that He sees. Which are way better than our own ideas anyway!

For those that are not saved, this shows them an image of just how loving and kind our God truly is. Which in return may soften their heart to learning and loving the one, true, amazing God. Which would lead to their salvation and them living in eternal glory with Him.

God is not done with you. He has such amazing plans for you that even you can't fully fathom how truly amazing they are. This is one subject that is so near and dear to my heart because growing up I struggled so much with how much I mattered. I was bullied a bit in school, mostly for standing up for the other kids and then for my Christianity. Which in reality, drew me even closer to Christ.

Then my dad walked out on us when I was 18 and changed how I looked at myself some. I mean, how much did I matter if one of the people who was supposed to love me forever didn't? It brought years of questioning myself and truly finding my identity in Christ. I compared myself way too much and don't think that I truly understood how God could love me even if I made mistakes.

It wasn't until I was in my early twenties that I started truly seeking all that I was in God and took the steps of finding my true identity in Him. Not just that, but also realizing how much God truly loves me. How, no matter what, I am more precious than the most valuable jewels to Him. He always has His arms stretched wide ready for me to run into them.

Then, when I got diagnosed with cancer, I got a whole other look on life. Just how valuable it is, how we can't take our calling for granted or waste any time fulfilling what God has for us.

I knew in my heart that I was going to make it through this, God healed me two thousand years ago by sending His son to die for me on the cross. However, when something like this happens to you, it opens your eyes to so many things.

It shows you to love those around you all day, everyday. To tell those you love how much you do. To shine the light of God all day, everywhere you go. To make sure that you are a true follower of Christ, not the world. To make sure that you are truly following the calling God has for you, not the one you have for yourself.

Once you realize that God has an amazing plan for your life, you become unstoppable. You become a force to be reckoned with and as long as you stay focused on God, you won't lose. God always wins, and this battle called life is God's to fight and ours to obey Him through.

> "For my thoughts are not your thoughts, neither are your ways my ways," declares the Lord. "As the heavens are higher than the earth, so are my ways higher than your ways and my thoughts than your thoughts."
>
> —Isaiah 55:8-9 (NIV)

Even when we think we've got the plan all figured out, we don't unless we asked Him specifically for the answers. It's so funny that we think we know what we're doing, when in reality we have no clue. So many things are beyond us and our way of thinking, this is why we must follow the One who knows it all. The One who holds the world in His hands.

We must sacrifice our own fleshly desires and give into the ones that God so desperately wants us to have. He has so much more for you than you could ever think or imagine.

We must take it one step at a time, or we would get over-whelmed. This is why we typically only get one word or step at a time. Which is where our faith comes in, do we trust God in the next step even though we don't see the whole staircase?

Where your heart is, is where your mind stays. When our hearts are fixed on God, that allows our minds to be open to His will, His path, His way. The blessings of the Lord chase us down, which is why we must stay on the path that the Lord has for us. When we are on His path, following His way, bless-ings chase us down and we run right into some too!

He has so many great and amazing things planned for you and me, all He asks us to do is seek Him in the process. We must turn our hearts towards Him and only then can we truly see the greatness of our God.

Time Management

This is a subject that I think most can relate to. Time management... How *do* you do it? I do have to say that I have yet to master this one. I want to say that I am perfect in this and don't have anymore to learn, but that would be farthest from the truth. This subject is one I continue to learn about daily.

Throughout my journey this past year, this has been a topic I've learned more and more about. Working from home and running my own business already put obstacles in front of me. Learning when to shut off work and be present with family, feeling like if I'm home I need to be working, and focusing on growing my business on top of all of that.

Then, throw in chemo. The chemo itself wasn't bad, it was only about five hours of my life every other Tuesday, plus an hour drive to and from. However, when you throw in the healing part and overcoming tired, that's when you realize that time management is so important.

Part of time management is realizing the different aspects of it. Yes, it's balancing work with family, but it's so much more than that. It's also balancing your time, friend time, routines, health, feeding yourself (don't forget that one, it's important), and most importantly, time with God.

We can get so caught up in all that we "must" do and forget to spend time with the one who made us so we could do all of those things. When managing our time, the most important thing we can do is seek the Lord. He is the one who knows the beginning to the end, so who better to have in charge of your schedule?

> Teach us to number our days, that we may gain a heart of wisdom.
>
> —Psalm 90:12 (NIV)

> If any of you lacks wisdom, you should ask God, who gives generously to all without finding fault, and it will be given to you.
>
> — James 1:5 (NIV)

After reading these two verses we can see that, even though we may not know what tomorrow holds, it is wise to remember that we are told to number our days and we must make the most out of them. When we come to this conclusion, it makes each day more special than the last.

When we think about our days and all they are to bring, we must bring God into the decision of what to do now. What steps to take, where to be, what to do. He has the ultimate authority in my life when it comes to these choices, and I hope He does in yours too.

God has knowledge way beyond what we could even think about. He knows how this life will end, He knows what tomorrow brings. Allow yourself to submit fully to the God of creation and open yourself up to the plans that He has for you, not your own.

> Look carefully then how you walk, not as unwise but as wise, making the best use of the time, because the days are evil. Therefore do not be foolish, but understand what the will of the Lord is.
>
> —Ephesians 5:15-17 (ESV)

The Lord even instructs us to be wise stewards of the time we are given. He knows that we have the choice to make wise or unwise calls, He gave us that choice. He just lays it out that we should make wise ones. I'm with Him.

This world is full of distractions and surrounds us with opportunities to do quite the opposite. We have chances everyday to open ourselves up to choices that could change the course of our lives as we know it.

God gave us free will and grace, that doesn't mean we should use everyday as an opportunity to do what we want and then repent about it later.

We are given the choice which path to walk, but Matthew

instructs us in which way to go.

> But small is the gate and narrow the road that leads to life,
> and only a few find it.
>
> —Matthew 7:14 (NIV)

Then, we can look in Isaiah 30:21 (NIV) which says,

> Whether you turn to the right or to the left, your ears will
> hear a voice behind you, saying, "This is the way; walk in
> it."

So we know which path to take, and we know that if we were to venture off or even think about it, there is a still small voice telling us to stay the course.

The key to making sure we take the right path is hearing from God—plain and simple. This is one reason we must open ourselves up to Him each day and spend quality time with the one who made us. He knows us better than anyone ever could.

He knows our hearts desires, He knows who we will marry, He even knows the names of our future children and how many there will be. I don't know about you, but that is someone I would trust with my entire life.

Jeremiah 29:11 (NIV) says that He has plans to give us a hope and a future. That should spark a light in anyone's heart who knows Him. God can do only good, so the plans He has for us must be spectacular.

When seeking out how we should manage our time, we should seek first and foremost what God has for us to do for Him. Only then will our time be managed rightly. His things come before ours, seek His kingdom above your own (Matthew 6:33 ESV). This is first and foremost on our time management to do list.

Second, we should ask what God has for us. We may have an abundance of things we'd like to do, but that doesn't mean we should. One reason being for safety reasons. If we aren't where we are supposed to be, God's hand of protection can be lifted off of us. Not only that, but His favor and mercy as well.

I do not want a day without those being upon me. The way to keep them on you is to follow along the path that God has for you. Allow His hand in anything and everything pertaining to your life.

When you open this door for Him to walk through, you can withstand any trial, stand strong through any circumstance. With God on your side, you can't fail.

When I truly realized this last year that I needed to change something, there was one main thing that set me free. God spoke to my heart and said, "you have tomorrow." It was only then that I realized that not everything has to get done today.

Each day we must seek out what God would like for us to fulfill and do, then be at peace with doing the rest another day.

Only He truly knows what each day holds and therefore what we should do each day. He's way smarter than us, so we need to trust His Word in each and everything we do.

Run to Him today and seek Him in what areas of your life to keep and what to weed out. Let Him work in you and through you today for a truly satisfying life.

Take Care of You

This right here...*Oh man,* it's taken me so long to get to the point of actually doing this. Growing up and then entering into my twenties, I didn't realize the importance of self care. It wasn't something that was on the top of my mind.

I am what one would call an empath. Not in the weird way the world has made it out to be, but in the godly sense. I can feel others emotions and tend to take them on. I gravitate towards helping others and always want to make sure others are taken care of and would never want to do anything to hurt someone's feelings. Thinking that someone is hurt because of me breaks my heart.

I grew up being bullied in school because I always stood up for those who wouldn't or couldn't stand up for themselves. My top giving love language is gifts and close behind is words of affirmation, so I am always giving gifts to those I care about and love to send daily texts or reminders of how loved they are.

Growing up and even now, my life has been about others.

Personally, I wouldn't have it any other way. My more sensitive personality has had a big part of who I am today and I wouldn't trade it for the world.

For the longest time I wasn't quite sure if being an empath was a gift or just made my life harder. I now realize that it is truly a gift, just one that we must learn to control and not let it control us. God gave me this special gift as a way to use me throughout my life to fulfill His plan. With that being said, I am totally thankful for what He has called me to do. I don't know of too many people who have the empath gift on this level, so I do understand the importance of what God has called me to do.

I don't say this all to brag on myself or show you what I can do, I say it to prove to you that I have had quite the time learning to take care of me.

When thinking about doing something for myself, I always saw it as selfish. If I did it for me, shouldn't I be doing it for someone else instead? Aren't we called to put others needs above our own and always be doing for God's people?

The answer is yes, however, you still matter too.

Do you not know that your bodies are temples of the Holy Spirit, who is in you, whom you have received from God? You are not your own; you were bought at a price. Therefore honor God with your bodies.

—1 Corinthians 6:19-20 (NIV)

God bought us with a price, the death of His son on the cross. To God we matter more than you could ever know. To not care about ourselves is honestly a disgrace to God, our Creator. He took His time making sure that every detail of us is perfectly perfect in every way. He makes sure to keep track of the number of hairs on our heads. He laughs when we laugh, He cries when we cry. God cares so much about us, so it's time to start caring about ourselves too.

> Since you are precious and honored in my sight, and because I love you, I will give people in exchange for you, nations in exchange for your life.
>
> —Isaiah 43:4 (NIV)

Heaven is paved with gold and the entrance is a giant pearl. God, the One who owns the world and created our very being, thinks that we are precious. He thinks of us higher than any stone or jewel there ever was. He knows us each by name before we are even born. He is incredible beyond belief and He loves us. We are precious in His sight.

If that doesn't touch your heart beyond words I don't know what will. God is a glorious being who could have anything He ever wanted, and He chose us.

When we don't love ourselves, we are denying God glory for His handiwork. This is honestly such a harsh thing to do to the one who made us.

When we choose to love ourselves and acknowledge all that God has made us to be, we choose to give Him credit for making such intricate and amazing beings.

This can be done in the simplest of ways. Choosing to take time for yourself to refresh, going to get you a cup of coffee and walking around your favorite store, buying you the top that you feel pretty in, getting your hair done, going fishing, just spending time reading the Word. There are so many ways to show yourself self care, you just have to pick what's right for you. You just have to find what's right for you and what makes you come alive again. Find what draws you closer to God and encourages your walk with Him.

Another helpful tool is finding a good faith buddy who you can talk with no matter what. One who won't judge you but will love you and build you up through everything life throws at you.

You are worth more than rubies, you are priceless. Let God's love surround you today, feel His embrace. Then, love yourself and all that He's made you to be.

Scriptures

HOPE

"For I know the plans I have for you," declares the Lord, "plans to prosper you and not to harm you, plans to give you hope and a future."

—Jeremiah 29:11 (NIV)

"Why, my soul, are you downcast? Why so disturbed within me?Put your hope in God, for I will yet praise him, my Savior and my God."

—Psalm 42:11 (NIV)

But those who hope in the Lord will renew their strength. They will soar on wings like eagles; they will run and not grow weary, they will walk and not be faint.

—Isaiah 40:31 (NIV)

May the God of hope fill you with all joy and peace as you trust in him, so that you may overflow with hope by the power of the Holy Spirit.

—Romans 15:13 (NIV)

GOD'S GOODNESS

And he passed in front of Moses, proclaiming, "The Lord, the Lord, the compassionate and gracious God, slow to anger, abounding in love and faithfulness…"

—Exodus 34:6 (NIV)

Give thanks to the Lord, for he is good; his love endures forever.

—1 Chronicles 16:34 (NIV)

Surely your goodness and love will follow me all the days of my life; and I will dwell in the house of the Lord forever.

—Psalm 23:6 (NIV)

I remain confident of this: I will see the goodness of the Lord in the land of the living.

—Psalm 27:13 (NIV)

Let them give thanks to the Lord for his unfailing love and His wonderful deeds for mankind, for he satisfies the thirsty and fills the hungry with good things.

—Psalm 107:8-9 (NIV)

BLESSINGS

And my God will meet all your needs according to the riches of his glory in Christ Jesus. To our God and Father be glory for ever and ever. Amen.

—Philippians 4:19-20 (NIV)

The Lord bless you and keep you; the Lord make his face shine on you and be gracious to you; the Lord turn his face toward you and give you peace.

—Numbers 6:24-26 (NIV)

And God is able to bless you abundantly, so that in all things at all times, having all that you need, you will abound in every good work. As it is written: "They have freely scattered their gifts to the poor; their righteousness endures forever." Now he who supplies seed to the sower and bread for food will also supply and increase your store of seed and will enlarge the harvest of your righteousness.

—2 Corinthians 9:8-10 (NIV)

FINANCES

"Bring the whole tithe into the storehouse, that there may be food in my house. Test me in this," says the Lord Almighty, "and see if I will not throw open the floodgates of heaven and pour out so much blessing that there will not be room enough to store it."

—Malachi 3:10 (NIV)

But remember the Lord your God, for it is he who gives you the ability to produce wealth, and so confirms his covenant, which he swore to your ancestors, as it is today.

—Deuteronomy 8:18 (NIV)

And my God will meet all your needs according to the riches of his glory in Christ Jesus.

—Philippians 4:19 (NIV)

"Keep this Book of the Law always on your lips; meditate on it day and night, so that you may be careful to do everything written in it. Then you will be prosperous and successful."

—Joshua 1:8 (NIV)

And God is able to bless you abundantly, so that in all things at all times, having all that you need, you will abound in every good work.

—2 Corinthians 9:8 (NIV)

DON'T GIVE UP

I have fought the good fight, I have finished the race, I have kept the faith.

—2 Timothy 4:7 (NIV)

He gives strength to the weary and increases the power of the weak. Even youths grow tired and weary, and young men stumble and fall; but those who hope in the Lord will renew their strength. They will soar on wings like eagles; they will run and not grow weary, they will walk and not be faint.

—Isaiah 40:29-31 (NIV)

Let us not become weary in doing good, for at the proper time we will reap a harvest if we do not give up.

—Galations 6:9 (NIV)

Blessed is the one who perseveres under trial because, having stood the test, that person will receive the crown of life that the Lord has promised to those who love him.

—James 1:12 (NIV)

No discipline seems pleasant at the time, but painful. Later on, however, it produces a harvest of righteousness and peace for those who have been trained by it.

—Hebrews 12:11 (NIV)

YOU ARE LOVED

Do everything in love.

—1 Corinthians 16:4 (NIV)

Above all, love each other deeply, because love covers over a multitude of sins.

—1 Peter 4:8 (NIV)

"Greater love has no one than this: to lay down one's life for one's friends."

—John 15:13 (NIV)

And now these three remain: faith, hope and love. But the greatest of these is love.

—1 Corinthians 13:13 (NIV)

THE LOVE OF GOD

For God so loved the world that He gave his one and only Son, that whoever believes in Him shall not perish but have eternal life.

—John 3:16 (NIV)

This is how God showed his love among us: He sent his one and only Son into the world that we might live through him. This is love: not that we loved God, but that he loved us and sent his Son as an atoning sacrifice for our sins. Dear friends, since God so loved us, we also ought to love one another.

—1 John 4:9-11 (NIV)

No, in all these things we are more than conquerors through him who loved us. For I am convinced that neither death nor life, neither angels nor demons, neither the present nor the future, nor any powers, neither height nor depth, nor anything else in all creation, will be able to separate us from the love of God that is in Christ Jesus our Lord.

—Romans 8:37-39 (NIV)

But God demonstrates his own love for us in this: While we

were still sinners, Christ died for us.

—Romans 5:8 (NIV)

"I have been crucified with Christ and I no longer live, but Christ lives in me. The life I now live in the body, I live by faith in the Son of God, who loved me and gave himself for me."

—Galatians 2:20 (NIV)

YOU MATTER

"For I know the plans I have for you," declares the Lord, "plans to prosper you and not to harm you, plans to give you hope and a future."

—Jeremiah 29:11 (NIV)

"For I am the Lord your God who takes hold of your right hand and says to you, Do not fear; I will help you."

—Isaiah 41:13 (NIV)

For you created my inmost being; you knit me together in my mother's womb.

—Psalm 139:13 (NIV)

"Before I formed you in the womb I knew you, before you were born I set you apart; I appointed you as a prophet to the nations."

—Jeremiah 1:5 (NIV)

TIME MANAGEMENT

Be very careful, then, how you live—not as unwise but as wise, making the most of every opportunity, because the days are evil. Therefore do not be foolish, but understand what the Lord's will is.

—Ephesians 5:15-17 (NIV)

Be wise in the way you act toward outsiders; make the most of every opportunity.

—Colossians 4:5 (NIV)

Teach us to number our days, that we may gain a heart of wisdom.

—Psalm 90:12 (NIV)

If any of you lacks wisdom, you should ask God, who gives generously to all without finding fault, and it will be given to you.

—James 1:5 (NIV)

TAKING CARE OF YOU

Do you not know that your bodies are temples of the Holy Spirit, who is in you, whom you have received from God? You are not your own; you were bought at a price. Therefore honor God with your bodies.

—1 Corinthians 6:19-20 (NIV)

Don't you know that you yourselves are God's temple and that God's Spirit dwells in your midst? If anyone destroys God's temple, God will destroy that person; for God's temple is sacred, and you together are that temple.

—1 Corinthians 3:16-17 (NIV)

Therefore, I urge you, brothers and sisters, in view of God's mercy, to offer your bodies as a living sacrifice, holy and pleasing to God—this is your true and proper worship.

—Romans 12:1 (NIV)

Daily Confessions

HEALTH

I will never be sick another day of my life.

With long life He will satisfy me.

All my organs function as God made them.

My white blood cell count is normal.

All my tests come back clean and clear.

I am strong in the Lord and in the power of His might.

Everything in my body functions the way it should.

I never have any negative side effects.

I am the healed and the whole.

I shall live and declare the works of the Lord.

My body is strong.

FINANCES

All my bills are paid for.

I have extra coming in.

I am paying everything off quickly.

Chips and chunks are coming in.

My God supplies all my needs according to HIS riches in glory by Christ Jesus.

My finances are strong.

People hand me money everyday.

I have seed coming in.

I am always led in my finances.

People always send me checks in the mail.

My debts are reduced and eliminated.

God is my source.

Everything I put my hand to prospers.

EVERYDAY CONFESSIONS

I have million dollar ideas.

I hear God's voice.

God has great plans for me.

My business is taking off.

God's favor surrounds me as with a shield.

God's favor goes before me.

God's blessings chase me down.

I am led by God.

I always hear His voice.

His peace surrounds me.

God is on my side.

I am blessed and highly favored.

I encourage you to use your words to benefit your life, not to harm it. Use these confessions as a baseline for speaking life into your life!

CALL TO SALVATION

If you declare with your mouth, "Jesus is Lord," and believe in your heart that God raised him from the dead, you will be saved. For it is with your heart that you believe and are justified, and it is with your mouth that you profess your faith and are saved.

—Romans 10:9-10 (NIV)

If you are not saved, or have wandered away from God, I encourage you to read this allowed and ask Jesus into your heart right now. It will not only change your life while here on this earth, but it will guarantee your eternal life with Christ. As you pray this, believe in your heart and you will be saved.

Repeat After Me:

"I, ___, invite you Jesus to live in my heart today. I believe that you are the son of God and that you died on the cross for me. I believe that God raised you from the dead. Jesus, you are my Lord and I promise to serve you all the days of my life."

Afterword

I am pleased to write that in April of 2021 my bills were reduced! The hospital said that they couldn't help financially, but God showed off big time. They reduced my bills by ninety-five percent and God is bringing in the rest!

I am finished with chemo and I am cancer free! Healed and whole. No lingering side effects, nothing!

I'm finishing strong and with faith that can move a mountain! Don't give up, keep going, and run this race. The strongest pressure comes right before the biggest breakthroughs.

About the Author

Sabrina Wages is a professional photographer and graphic designer who runs and operates her own businesses. Throughout Sabrina's career as a business owner, she has strived to shine the light of Christ through every product and service she provides.

Sabrina is one of seven children, the five younger being adopted. Sabrina is also a cancer overcomer, who was declared cancer free in 2020. She overcame Hodgkins Lymphoma with six cycles of chemo (two treatments in each cycle). Sabrina stayed the course and came out stronger than she was before! Having her faith tested, she persevered and grew strong in her relationship with Christ.

As a Christian, Sabrina's faith is her most important attribute. She attends Faith Life Church in Branson, Missouri where she serves on their children's team.

Sabrina is looking forward to one day soon becoming a wife and mother to those God has for her. Being a momma is a calling God has placed on her life.

Though writing a book wasn't ever at the top of Sabrina's to do list, she is so thankful that God opened this door and changed that. She reminds us all to go with God's plan for our lives, not our own. She hopes that through this book you found the peace and hope that you need to fulfill this journey that God has for you.

CPSIA information can be obtained
at www.ICGtesting.com
Printed in the USA
BVHW041032280821
615448BV00017B/650